Unveiling Google Gemini AI

Decoding the Secrets, Applications, and Future Impact of Multimodal Brilliance

DE GIST LOVERS

Table of contents

Preface

The field of artificial intelligence has witnessed remarkable progress in recent years, with large language models (LLMs) emerging as a driving force. Among these LLMs, Gemini AI stands out for its impressive capabilities in text generation, translation, code writing, and more. This book aims to delve into the inner workings of Gemini AI, providing a comprehensive and technical understanding of its architecture, algorithms, and training data.

Target Audience

This book is intended for readers with a technical background in computer science or artificial intelligence. It assumes a basic understanding of machine learning, deep learning, and natural language processing (NLP) concepts. However, even if you are not an expert in these areas, the book provides sufficient introductory information to follow the discussion.

Part 1:
Foundations of Large Language Models

In the dynamic landscape of artificial intelligence, Large Language Models (LLMs) have emerged as pivotal entities, shaping the way machines comprehend and generate human-like language. This chapter provides a broad yet insightful overview of LLMs, charting their historical development and exploring their current applications.

The journey of LLMs traces back to the early days of natural language processing and machine learning. Initially conceived as rule-based systems, early language models struggled to capture the intricacies of human language. The breakthrough, however, came with the advent of statistical approaches and the utilization of vast corpora of text data.

As we progressed into the era of deep learning, the introduction of neural networks, particularly recurrent neural networks (RNNs) and long short-term memory (LSTM) networks, marked a significant leap in language understanding. These models paved the way for more complex architectures, setting the stage for the Transformer model, a cornerstone in the development of contemporary LLMs.

The present-day applications of LLMs span a diverse array of fields, demonstrating their versatility and impact. In natural language processing, models like OpenAI's GPT series and Google's BERT have become instrumental in tasks such as sentiment analysis, language translation, and question answering.

Beyond textual domains, LLMs have extended their reach into image captioning, summarization, and even code generation. The ability to process and generate coherent and contextually relevant content has positioned these models as invaluable tools across various industries.

The widespread adoption of LLMs signifies a paradigm shift in the capabilities of AI systems. These models, by leveraging vast amounts of data, have attained a level of language understanding that enables them to generate contextually rich and context-aware responses. This evolution has profound implications for communication, information retrieval, and the development of more sophisticated AI applications.

<u>Key concepts such as tokenization, word embedding, and attention mechanisms.</u>

To comprehend the inner workings of Large Language Models (LLMs) like Gemini AI, it's crucial to delve into key concepts that form the bedrock of language understanding. This chapter will unravel the intricacies of tokenization, word embedding, and attention mechanisms, providing a foundational understanding of these pivotal concepts.

Tokenization is the process of breaking down textual content into smaller units, known as tokens. These tokens can be as granular as individual characters or as broad as entire words or phrases. In the realm of language models, the choice of tokenization plays a crucial role in determining how effectively the model can capture and understand the nuances of language.

For instance, in English, tokenizing a sentence like "Machine learning is fascinating!" might result in individual tokens such as ["Machine", "learning", "is", "fascinating", "!"]. This granular breakdown facilitates the model's ability to process and analyze language at a more detailed level.

Word embedding involves representing words as numerical vectors in a multi-dimensional space. This representation aims to capture the semantic relationships between words based on their contextual usage. Rather than treating words as isolated entities, word embedding enables the model to understand their meanings in relation to surrounding words.

Imagine a geometric space where the distance and direction between word vectors reflect the semantic similarities and relationships between words. This contextualization allows models like Gemini AI to grasp the intricate nuances of language and generate more contextually relevant responses.

Attention mechanisms serve as a spotlight in language models, enabling them to focus on specific parts of input sequences when generating output. This mechanism allows the model to assign varying degrees of importance to different words in a sequence, enhancing its ability to capture long-range dependencies and relationships.

In essence, attention mechanisms simulate how humans pay attention to specific words when comprehending language. By dynamically adjusting the weights assigned to each word during processing, attention mechanisms empower models to prioritize the most relevant information, contributing to more accurate and contextually aware language understanding.

Part 2:
Unveiling the Architecture of Gemini AI

Gemini AI's architecture, examining its components and interactions

At the heart of Gemini AI lies the Transformer model, a revolutionary architecture that has reshaped the landscape of natural language processing. This model's transformative power stems from its ability to process sequential data while considering the entire context, overcoming limitations present in earlier models.

The Transformer model employs a mechanism known as self-attention, enabling it to weigh the significance of different words in a sequence concerning each other. This mechanism is pivotal for capturing long-range dependencies in language, a feat that contributes significantly to Gemini AI's exceptional language understanding capabilities.

Within the Transformer model, two fundamental components play distinctive roles — the encoder and the decoder. The encoder processes input sequences, extracting essential features and representations. Simultaneously, the decoder generates output sequences based on the encoded information. This modular approach enhances the model's flexibility and adaptability across diverse language tasks.

Building upon the foundation of attention mechanisms, Gemini AI's architecture strategically employs attention layers within both the encoder and decoder. These layers allow the model to focus on specific parts of input and output sequences, facilitating a nuanced understanding of language nuances and contextual dependencies.

Beyond the conceptual brilliance of its architecture, Gemini AI undergoes meticulous optimization to ensure optimal performance. Techniques like parameter tuning, regularization, and advanced optimization algorithms contribute to refining the model's accuracy and efficiency.

The seamless interaction between components is a hallmark of Gemini AI's architecture. As input sequences traverse through the encoder, critical information is distilled, forming a rich representation that the decoder utilizes to generate contextually relevant and coherent outputs. This dynamic interplay empowers Gemini AI to excel in tasks ranging from text generation to code writing.

The Transformer model, core building blocks, and optimizations

Within the intricate tapestry of Gemini AI's architecture lies the transformative power of the renowned Transformer model. In this chapter, we embark on a detailed exploration, unraveling the core building blocks and optimizations that define the very essence of Gemini AI's unparalleled language processing capabilities.

The Essence of Transformation

At the heart of Gemini AI's architecture resides the Transformer model, a revolutionary paradigm in the realm of natural language processing. Let's dissect its core building blocks and understand how they contribute to the model's extraordinary capabilities.

1. Self-Attention Mechanism

The transformative power of the Transformer model emanates from its ingenious use of the self-attention mechanism. Unlike its predecessors, this mechanism enables Gemini AI to weigh the importance of each word in a sequence concerning every other word. This holistic perspective is pivotal for capturing intricate linguistic nuances and dependencies, setting

Gemini AI apart in the landscape of language models.

2. Multi-Head Attention

To further enhance its capacity for capturing diverse patterns, the Transformer model employs multi-head attention. This involves running the self-attention mechanism in parallel across multiple "heads," allowing the model to consider different aspects of the input sequence simultaneously. The fusion of insights from these multiple perspectives enriches the model's understanding and fosters a more nuanced representation of language.

3. Positional Encoding

Given that the Transformer model inherently lacks information about the order of tokens in a sequence, positional encoding becomes crucial. Gemini AI strategically incorporates positional encoding to infuse the model with the positional information necessary for understanding the sequential structure of language.

Optimization for Precision

Beyond its conceptual brilliance, Gemini AI's Transformer model undergoes meticulous optimization to elevate its performance to unprecedented levels. These optimizations include:

1. Parameter Tuning

Fine-tuning the model's parameters is an iterative process, where the intricacies of its internal configurations are adjusted to achieve optimal performance. This ensures that Gemini AI aligns with the specific demands of the tasks it undertakes.

2. Regularization Techniques

To prevent overfitting and enhance generalization, Gemini AI integrates regularization techniques. These mechanisms, such as dropout, contribute to a more robust model that excels across diverse datasets.

3. Advanced Optimization Algorithms

The model leverages sophisticated optimization algorithms that fine-tune its parameters during the training process. These algorithms, including variants of stochastic gradient descent, ensure that Gemini AI converges efficiently to optimal solutions.

Role of different layers, including encoder, decoder, and attention mechanisms

Within Gemini AI's sophisticated architecture, a symphony of components collaborates seamlessly to decipher the complexities of language. In this chapter, we illuminate the roles played by the encoder, decoder, and attention mechanisms, unraveling the intricate layers that orchestrate Gemini AI's language understanding.

THE ENCODER

At the forefront of language comprehension, the encoder takes raw input and transforms it into a format that the model can interpret.

Within Gemini AI, the encoder's duties are multifaceted:

Token Embedding: The encoder begins by converting input tokens into vectors, a process known as token embedding. This initial transformation lays the groundwork for subsequent layers to extract nuanced information.

Positional Encoding: As language inherently carries sequential nuances, the encoder incorporates positional encoding to maintain the contextual order of tokens. This step ensures that Gemini AI grasps the sequential flow of language, a pivotal aspect of its proficiency.

Multi-Head Self-Attention: In the spirit of Gemini AI's innovative architecture, the encoder employs multi-head self-attention. This mechanism allows the model to weigh the significance of each word in the input sequence concerning others, capturing intricate dependencies.

THE DECODER

While the encoder sets the stage, the decoder takes center stage in crafting meaningful and coherent responses. Key responsibilities of the decoder include:

Token Embedding and Positional Encoding: Similar to the encoder, the decoder initiates the process with token embedding and positional encoding. This ensures that the model retains an understanding of sequential context during the response generation phase.

Masked Self-Attention: To prevent the model from "peeking" at future tokens during training, the decoder employs masked self-attention. This strategic mechanism contributes to the generation of responses that align with the sequential flow of the conversation.

Multi-Head Encoder-Decoder Attention: In fostering a comprehensive understanding, the decoder leverages multi-head attention to capture insights from different parts of the input sequence. This collaborative process enhances the model's ability to generate contextually relevant responses.

At the core of Gemini AI's language symphony lies attention mechanisms. These mechanisms orchestrate the allocation of focus, enabling the model to discern the salience of different elements. The harmony of attention mechanisms ensures a nuanced and contextually aware interpretation of language, empowering Gemini AI to excel in diverse linguistic tasks.

Part 3:

Demystifying the Training Process

The training process of Gemini AI

Embarking on the journey to understand Gemini AI's unparalleled language proficiency, we delve into the intricate realm of its training process. Like a maestro fine-tuning an instrument, Gemini undergoes meticulous training rituals, shaping its linguistic virtuosity.

Crafting Intelligence from Diversity

- Datasets as the Crucible: At the heart of Gemini AI's training lies a diverse array of datasets. These datasets, akin to the notes in a musical composition, encompass a vast spectrum of linguistic nuances. Drawn from diverse sources, including books, articles, and online content, these datasets lay the foundation for Gemini's comprehensive language understanding.

- Tensor Processing Units (TPUs): In its training symphony, Gemini AI harmonizes with Google's Tensor Processing Units (TPUs). These specialized hardware accelerators, designed for machine learning workloads, empower Gemini to traverse the vast landscape of its training datasets with unprecedented speed and efficiency.

The Prelude: Pre-training

- Unveiling the Transformer: Before the grand performance, Gemini undergoes pre-training, a crucial phase in shaping its language comprehension. The Transformer model, a key architectural masterpiece, serves as the guiding light during this prelude. Gemini learns to predict missing words in sentences, fostering an innate understanding of language structures.

- The Masked Language Model (MLM): Akin to a musician refining their skills through practice, Gemini engages in the Masked Language Model (MLM) task. This entails predicting masked words within a sentence, enhancing the model's ability to infer contextual meaning and relationships between words.

The Crescendo: Fine-Tuning

- Specialized Fine-Tuning: As Gemini progresses through its pre-training, the journey crescendos into fine-tuning. This phase tailors the model to specific tasks, transforming it into a versatile virtuoso. Fine-tuning refines Gemini's capabilities for tasks like text generation, translation, and code writing, ensuring its adaptability across diverse applications.

- Domain-Specific Expertise: During fine-tuning, Gemini hones its expertise in specialized domains, such as computer vision, geospatial science, human health, and integrated technologies. This domain-specific refinement enhances Gemini's proficiency, allowing it to excel in a myriad of real-world scenarios.

The impact of data quality and diversity on model performance

In the orchestration of Gemini AI's language mastery, the impact of data quality and diversity emerges as a pivotal movement. This chapter unravels the symphony of data, illuminating how the composition of datasets plays a decisive role in shaping Gemini's performance.

Data Quality: The Conductor's Baton

- Pristine Notes of Precision: Much like a conductor demanding precision from each instrument, Gemini thrives on high-quality data. Pristine datasets free from noise and inaccuracies serve as the foundation for the model's linguistic finesse. The emphasis on data quality ensures that Gemini learns from reliable sources, fostering a robust understanding of language structures and semantics.

- Guardians of Integrity: Rigorous data quality checks act as guardians, ensuring that the training datasets mirror the richness of human language without distortions. The meticulous curation of data aligns with Gemini's pursuit of excellence, enhancing its ability to generate accurate and contextually relevant outputs.

Diversity: Harmonizing the Melody

- A Diverse Ensemble: Diversity in training datasets is the harmonious ensemble that enriches Gemini's linguistic repertoire. Drawing from a myriad of sources, genres, and styles, the model learns to navigate the complexities and subtleties of language. The diverse training landscape empowers Gemini to understand context, idioms, and cultural nuances, mirroring the intricacies of human communication.

- Cross-Pollination of Knowledge: Gemini's exposure to diverse datasets acts as a catalyst for cross-pollination of knowledge. By assimilating information from varied domains, the model gains a holistic perspective, transcending narrow confines and becoming adept at addressing a wide array of user queries and tasks.

The Virtuosity Unleashed

- Optimizing for Excellence: The impact of data quality and diversity is not merely a stylistic choice; it defines the virtuosity of Gemini AI. By optimizing for excellence in data, Gemini emerges as a linguistic virtuoso, capable of performing intricate linguistic tasks with precision and creativity.

Part 4:
Exploring the Capabilities of Gemini AI

The diverse applications

In the expansive landscape of artificial intelligence, Gemini AI emerges as a versatile powerhouse, reshaping the paradigm of large language models. This section unveils the multifaceted brilliance of Gemini, exploring its diverse applications across text generation, translation, code crafting, and question answering.

Text Generation

Gemini AI stands as a linguistic virtuoso, seamlessly crafting narratives that captivate and inform. From imaginative storytelling to informative content creation, Gemini's proficiency in text generation redefines the boundaries of creative expression and information dissemination.

Translation Mastery

Witness Gemini's linguistic finesse as it effortlessly translates across languages, bridging communication gaps and preserving the essence of the original content. Dive into Gemini's translation capabilities, where language becomes a tool for global connectivity, fostering understanding and collaboration.

Code Crafting:

For developers and coding enthusiasts, Gemini AI becomes a coding companion, translating human intent into executable code with creative precision. Explore how Gemini navigates the intricacies of algorithmic language, transforming complexity into a symphony of executable instructions.

Question Answering

Gemini's intelligence shines as it tackles a myriad of questions, providing accurate and insightful answers. Delve into scenarios where Gemini demonstrates an adept understanding of context, excelling in knowledge retrieval and delivering concise, relevant responses. Explore how Gemini redefines information retrieval in the realm of question-answering.

The potential future applications and impact on different industries

Imagine a world where the boundaries between technology and healthcare blur, giving rise to a new era of personalized wellness. In the not-so-distant future, Gemini AI is set to revolutionize the healthcare landscape, seamlessly integrating biosensors, reshaping preventative medicine, and offering personalized healthcare solutions. Picture a scenario where Gemini becomes the cornerstone of enhanced diagnostics, empowering individuals to take proactive control of their health.

As we journey further into the future, the urban landscape transforms into smart cities that harness the geospatial intelligence of Gemini AI. Urban planning takes a quantum leap with continuous monitoring and multisource data fusion, paving the way for resilient and intelligent infrastructure. Visualize a cityscape where Gemini's insights drive informed decision-making, optimizing resources and crafting a blueprint for sustainable urban development.

Industries on the cusp of change find a reliable ally in Gemini AI. The multifaceted language model propels decision-making processes to new heights, facilitating domain knowledge transfer, data fusion, and advanced decision-making across diverse sectors. Envision an industrial landscape where Gemini becomes synonymous with innovation, efficiency, and the driving force behind transformative changes.

But the impact doesn't stop there. The coding landscape itself undergoes a revolutionary shift, with AlphaCode 2 powered by Gemini AI taking the lead. The future of coding is redefined as Gemini enhances speed and cost-effectiveness, surpassing its predecessors. Witness a coding landscape where human ingenuity harmonizes with machine intelligence, setting the stage for a new era of creativity and efficiency.

This is not just a glimpse into the future; it's an immersive exploration of the potential applications of Gemini AI, where industries are not merely affected but transformed. The impact on healthcare, urban planning, decision-making, and coding is not speculative—it's a tangible evolution waiting to unfold, driven by the limitless possibilities that Gemini AI brings to the table. The journey into the future promises not just innovation but a complete reimagination of how industries operate, all guided by the unparalleled intelligence of Gemini AI.

Part 5:
Ethical Considerations and Future Directions

Ethical concerns, including bias, fairness, and transparency

In the realm of artificial intelligence, the ethical considerations surrounding language models have become a focal point of discussion, and Gemini AI is no exception. As we delve into the ethical landscape, the journey begins with a critical examination of biases inherent in large language models.

Gemini AI, while powerful, is not immune to biases. It's essential to unravel the intricacies, acknowledging the potential biases that may be ingrained in the model. The exploration extends beyond mere acknowledgment; it involves a commitment to addressing and rectifying biases to foster fairness and impartiality.

Fairness is not just an aspiration but a fundamental principle embedded in the ethical fabric of Gemini AI. How does the model treat different demographics? Does it exhibit fairness across varied socio-cultural contexts? These questions drive the discourse on ensuring that Gemini AI transcends biases and stands as a paragon of equitable treatment.

Transparency emerges as a cornerstone in the ethical framework. Users and stakeholders deserve clarity on how Gemini AI operates, makes decisions, and interprets data. Unveiling the model's inner workings becomes paramount, providing a transparent view that fosters trust and accountability.

The journey through ethical considerations is not a passive one. It's an active commitment to continuous improvement. Gemini AI, like any technological innovation, evolves, and with evolution comes the responsibility to mitigate ethical challenges. This involves staying vigilant, incorporating user feedback, and employing strategies that align with ethical best practices.

As we navigate the ethical frontiers with Gemini AI, the goal is not just to meet ethical standards but to set new benchmarks. The model becomes a beacon of responsible AI, not just by addressing biases, ensuring fairness, and fostering transparency, but by actively contributing to the ethical discourse in the broader landscape of artificial intelligence. The journey toward ethical excellence is not a destination; it's an ongoing commitment that defines the ethical compass guiding Gemini AI into the future.

Strategies for mitigating risks and ensuring responsible development and deployment

Embarking on the path of responsible AI development and deployment with Gemini AI involves a meticulous exploration of strategies to mitigate risks. The narrative unfolds with a proactive approach, acknowledging the potential challenges and charting a course that prioritizes responsible practices.

Risk mitigation in the context of Gemini AI begins with a comprehensive understanding of the model's capabilities and limitations. Users, developers, and stakeholders alike benefit from a transparent communication of these aspects. By delineating the boundaries of the model's proficiency, expectations align with reality, contributing to a more informed and responsible user experience.

The development phase becomes a pivotal arena for risk mitigation. Rigorous testing, validation, and scenario analyses serve as the first line of defense against potential pitfalls. It's not just about creating a powerful model; it's about sculpting a model that withstands scrutiny, operates reliably, and minimizes unforeseen challenges.

Continuous monitoring emerges as a cornerstone strategy. Gemini AI is not a static entity; it evolves with usage patterns and changing contexts. Implementing robust monitoring mechanisms ensures that any deviations or unexpected behaviors are promptly identified and addressed. This proactive stance prevents risks from escalating, fostering an ecosystem of trust and reliability.

User education becomes an integral part of risk mitigation. Empowering users with knowledge about Gemini AI's capabilities, its ethical considerations, and how to interact responsibly enhances the overall user experience. Education is not just about using the model; it's about cultivating a community of informed users who contribute to the responsible use of AI.

Collaboration with diverse stakeholders amplifies the effectiveness of risk mitigation strategies. Engaging with the AI community, regulatory bodies, and user groups fosters a collective effort to identify, assess, and address risks comprehensively. The collaborative approach ensures a holistic perspective that goes beyond individual biases and interests.

As we navigate the terrain of responsible development and deployment with Gemini AI, the emphasis is not just on avoiding pitfalls but on cultivating a culture of responsibility. Mitigating risks becomes a shared commitment, a collective endeavor to harness the power of Gemini AI for positive impact while safeguarding against potential challenges. In this journey, the strategies employed are not mere safeguards; they are the building blocks of a responsible AI ecosystem.

A look at the future of LLMs and their potential societal impact

The closing chapters of our journey through the landscape of Gemini AI invite us to gaze into the future, exploring the untapped potential and societal impact that awaits. The narrative unfolds not as a mere projection but as an insightful journey into the promises and challenges that large language models (LLMs) like Gemini AI usher into the world.

As we peer into the future, one of the key realms that unfolds is the democratization of knowledge and information. Large language models have the inherent ability to break down language barriers, offering a more inclusive and accessible information landscape. The potential to bridge gaps in education, facilitate cross-cultural communication, and democratize access to insights positions LLMs like Gemini as catalysts for positive societal change.

The evolution of communication takes center stage in our exploration. With advancements in natural language processing, LLMs pave the way for more nuanced and context-aware interactions. The prospect of fluid, human-like conversations with machines opens new avenues for seamless human-AI collaboration. This shift has the potential to redefine how we communicate, share ideas, and collaborate in the digital age.

The societal impact of LLMs extends its reach into the creative realms. From aiding in content creation to generating innovative solutions, the collaborative interplay between human creativity and machine intelligence charts a course for unprecedented possibilities. Gemini AI, with its multimodal capabilities, holds the promise of being a creative companion, augmenting human ingenuity in realms such as art, design, and content creation.

However, with these promises come the responsibilities of ethical deployment and mindful governance. The narrative takes a nuanced turn, delving into the importance of ethical considerations in steering the societal impact of LLMs. Addressing concerns related to bias, fairness, and accountability becomes paramount, ensuring that the benefits of AI are harnessed without perpetuating existing societal challenges.

The future, as we envision it, is not just a trajectory but a dynamic interplay of choices and actions. Our exploration of Gemini AI's potential societal impact serves not as a crystal ball, but as a compass guiding us to navigate the evolving landscape responsibly. It is an invitation to collectively shape a future where the fusion of human intelligence and AI augments the fabric of society, contributing to a more informed, connected, and inclusive world.

Conclusion

As we draw the curtains on this exploration into the intricate world of Gemini AI, a tapestry of knowledge and innovation unfolds before us. The journey embarked upon has been one of revelation, traversing the historical landscapes of large language models, unraveling the intricate architecture of Gemini AI, and peering into the boundless possibilities it ushers into the future.

At the heart of our odyssey lies the realization that Gemini AI is not just a technological marvel; it is a transformative force with the potential to reshape the way we interact, create, and navigate the digital realm. The foundational understanding of large language models, the intricacies of Gemini's architecture, and the dynamics of its training process serve as pillars upon which we've built a profound comprehension.

Our sojourn through the diverse applications of Gemini AI – from text generation and translation to code writing and question answering – has illuminated the multifaceted capabilities that render it a versatile companion in our digital endeavors. The spotlight on future horizons has sparked contemplation on the societal impact, ethical considerations, and the responsible deployment of large language models, amplifying our awareness as custodians of this technological frontier.

Yet, this book is not merely a compendium of facts and technicalities; it is an ode to the fusion of human ingenuity and artificial intelligence. It resonates with the promise of democratized knowledge, redefined communication, and a collaborative future where creativity knows no bounds.

As we bid farewell to these pages, let it be known that the journey does not end here. The trajectory of Gemini AI is dynamic, and our understanding, though enriched, is but a snapshot in the grand tapestry of AI evolution. The call to action echoes – to stay engaged, to be at the forefront of updates, and to actively contribute to the responsible evolution of technology.

In the vast cosmos of artificial intelligence, Gemini is a constellation illuminating our path. This book, a compass guiding through its brilliance, is an invitation to embrace the unknown, to be architects of the AI future, and to witness the unfolding chapters of innovation and discovery. As the curtain falls, may our curiosity persist, our minds remain open, and our journey into the realms of AI continues to unfold.